COUNTRY *Ladies*

Edited by Milton Okun

Contents

Compiled by Len Handler
Production: Daniel Rosenbaum; Rana Bernhardt
Art Direction: Rosemary Cappa-Jenkins
Director of Music: Mark Phillips

ISBN: 0-89524-819-0

Alphabetical Listing

Love Can Build A Bridge

Words and Music by
Paul Overstreet, Naomi Judd
and John Jarvis

* Recorded a half step lower.

all your hopes— are sink - ing,   let me show you what love—means.   Love can build a
                                                                                                  er. ___

bridge ___   be - tween your heart and   mine.___

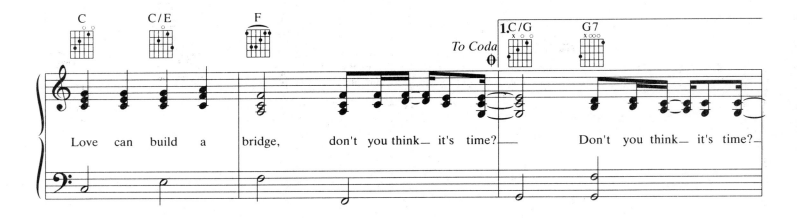

Love can build a   bridge,   don't you think— it's time?___   Don't you think— it's time?___

I would ___ Don't you think ___ it's time?

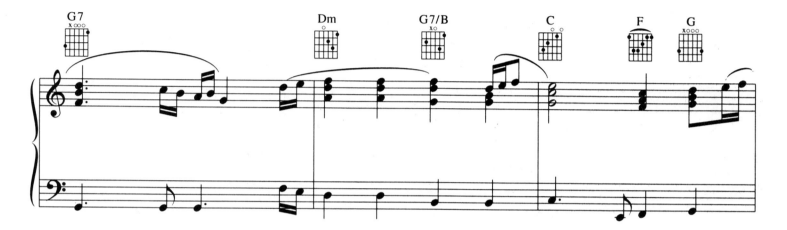

When we stand to-geth - er, ___ it's our fin - est hour. ___ We can do ___

D.S. al Coda

an - y-thing,_____ an - y-thing,_____ if we keep be-liev-in' in the pow-

Coda

_____ Don't you think_ it's time?_____

Yeah, yes I do._____ Love can build a

bridge be-tween your heart and mine._____

Love can build a bridge, don't you think_ it's time?_____ Don't you think_ it's time?_____

Additional Lyrics

2. I would whisper love so loudly,
   Every heart would understand
   That love and only love can
   Join the tribes of man.
   I would give my heart's desires
   So that you might see.
   The first step is to realize
   That it all begins with you and me. *(To Chorus)*

I Fall To Pieces

Words and Music by
Hank Cochran and Harlan Howard

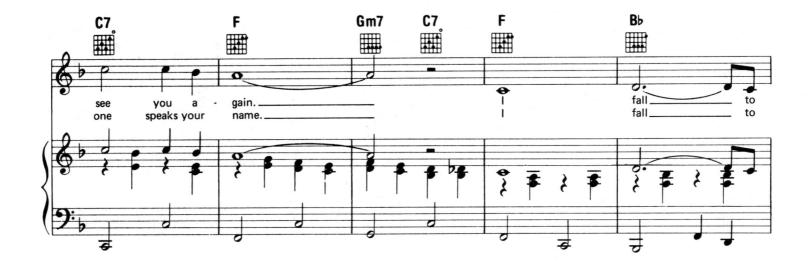

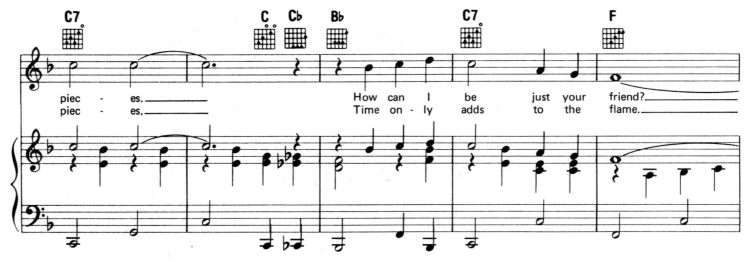

She Is His Only Need

Words and Music by
Dave Loggins

Bil - ly was a small town lon - er ___ who nev - er did dream ___

of ev - er leav-ing south-ern Ar - i - zo - na ___ or ev - er hear-ing wed-ding bells ___ ring.

He nev-er had a lot of luck with the la-dies, but he sure had a lot of good work-ing skills.

Nev-er cared a-bout climb-ing an-y lad-der.__ He knew the way in a small ca-fé. __ Found__

__ the will:__ he met Miss Bon-nie and a lit-tle bit of her was a lit-tle too much. __

A few mov-ies and a few months lat-er __ the feel-ing got strong e-nough. __

He did-n't own a car so it must have been love:

That drove him up-town for a dia-mond. That's when he start-ed go-in'

o-ver the line. Working o-ver-time

to give her things just to hear her say she don't de-serve 'em. But he loved her and he just kept

goin' o-ver-board, _____ o-ver the lim-it to af-ford____

to give her things he knew she want-ed. ____ 'Cause with-out her___ where_

__ would he _____ be?_____ See, it's not for him. ____

She is __ his on - ly _____ need.

Ring on her fin-ger and one __ on the lad - der. __

A new pro-mo-tion ev-'ry now and then. __ Bon-nie worked un - til she could-n't tie her ap-ron, then

stayed at home and had the first of two chil - dren. And my, how the time ___ did fly!

The ba - bies grew up and moved __ a - way. __ Left 'em sit-ting on the front porch rock-ing __ and

The Greatest Man I Never Knew

Words and Music by
Richard Leigh and Layng Martine, Jr.

Gently

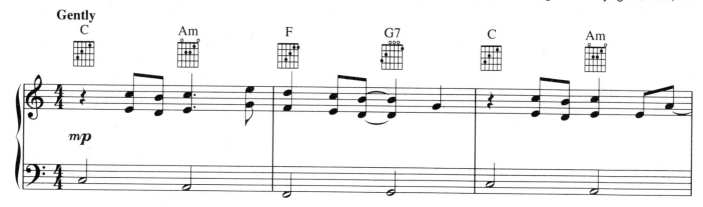

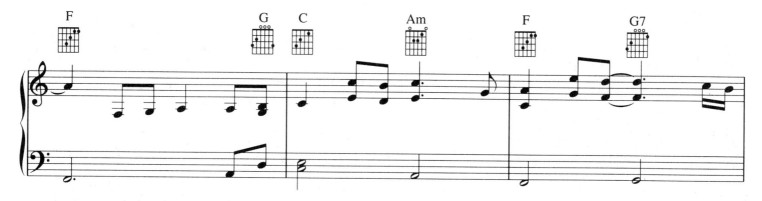

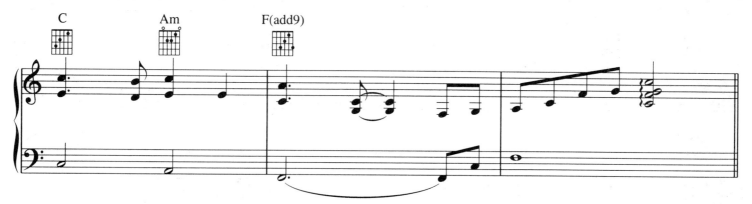

The great-est man I_____ nev - er knew_____ lived just down the hall,_____
The great-est man I_____ nev - er knew_____ came home late ev - 'ry night,_____
The great-est words I_____ nev - er heard_____ I guess I'll nev - er hear._____

and ev-'ry day we said ___ hel - lo ___
He nev-er had too much ___ to say.
The man I thought could nev - er die ___

but nev-er touched at all. ___
Too much was on his mind. ___
has been dead al-most a year. ___

He was in his pa -
I nev-er real - ly knew ___
Oh, he was good at bus -

- per.
___ him,
- 'ness

oh, and
but there was bus - 'ness left ___ to ___ do.

I was in my ___ room.
now it seems so ___ sad.

How was I to know ___ he thought I hung the ___ moon?
Ev - 'ry-thing he gave ___ to us took all he ___ had.
He nev - er said he loved ___ me. Guess he

To Coda ⊕

20

Passionate Kisses

Words and Music by
Lucinda Williams

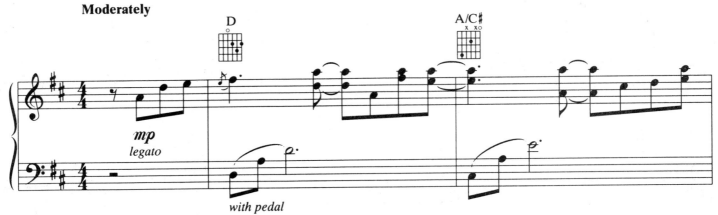

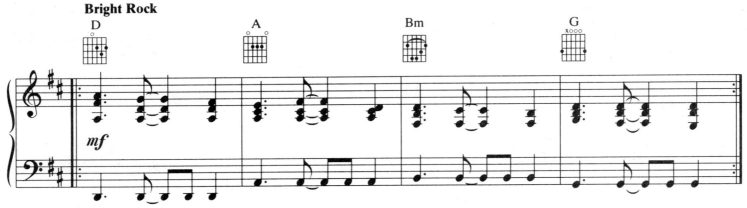

Is___ it too much to ask?___ I want a com-fort-a-ble bed___ that won't
Is___ it too much to de-mand?___ I want a full house___ and a

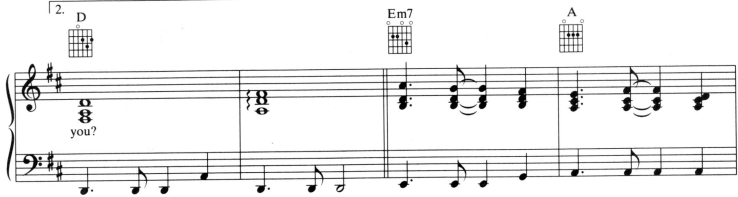

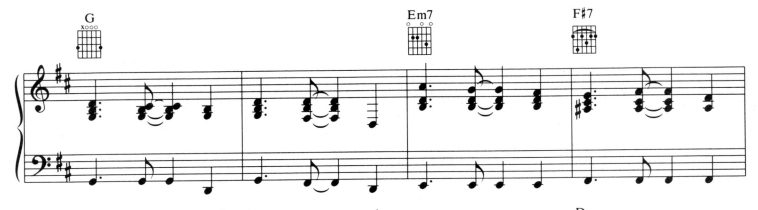

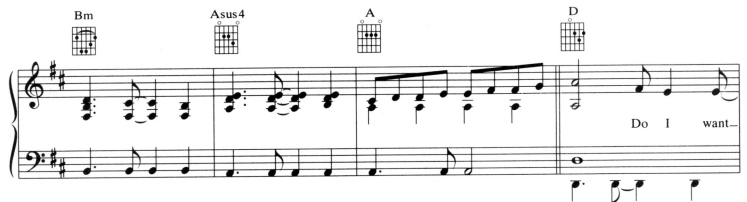

Do I want—

— too much?— Am I go - ing o - ver-board to want— that touch?—

I shout it out to the night.___ Give me what I de-serve,___ 'cause

D.S. al Coda

it's my right.___

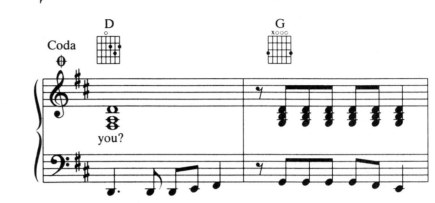

Coda

you?

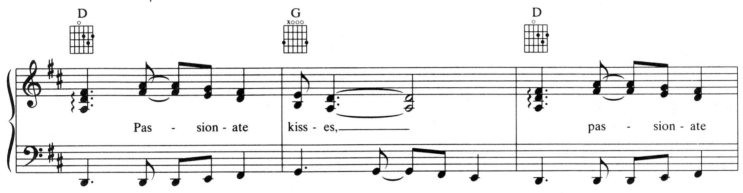

Pas - sion-ate kiss - es,___ pas - sion - ate

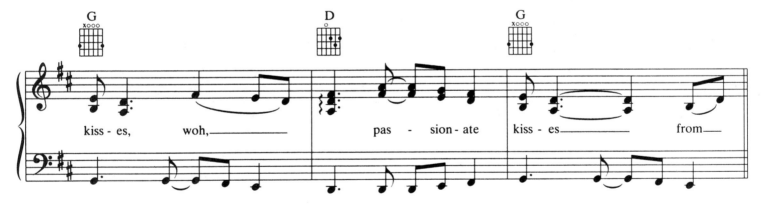

kiss - es, woh,___ pas - sion-ate kiss - es___ from___

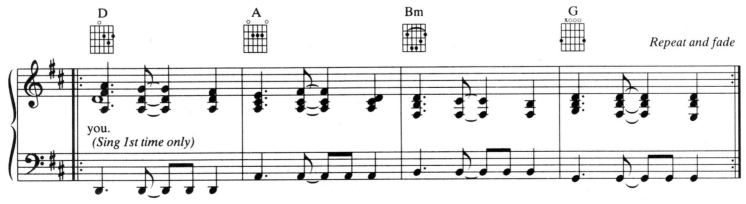

you.
(Sing 1st time only)

Repeat and fade

My Arms Stay Open All Night

Words and Music by
Paul Overstreet and Don Schlitz

Easy Country feel

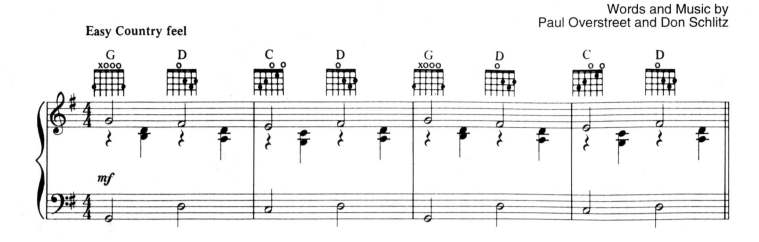

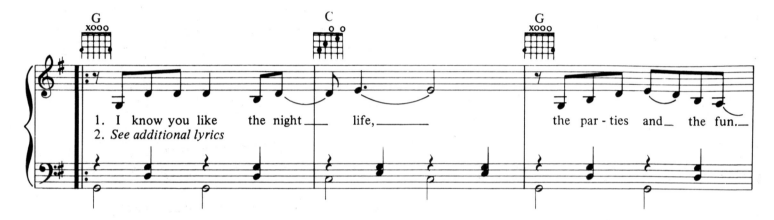

1. I know you like the night life, the par-ties and the fun.
2. *See additional lyrics*

You like to hang a-round un-til the

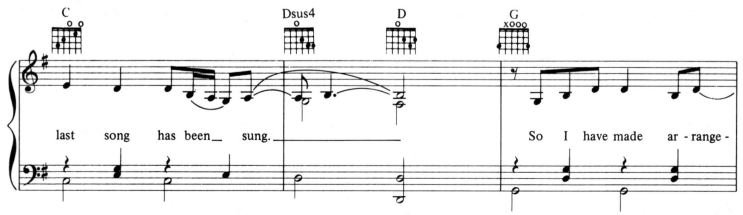

last song has been sung. So I have made ar-range-

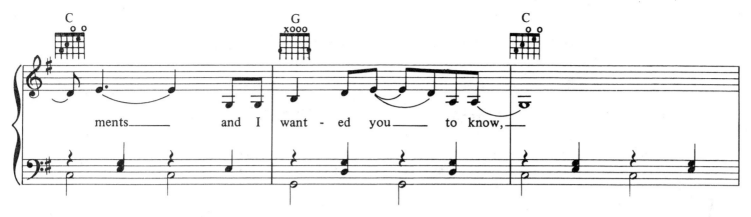

ments_____ and I want - ed you____ to know,____

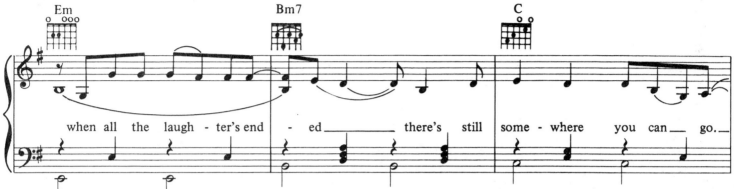

when all the laugh - ter's end - ed_____ there's still some - where you can_ go.___

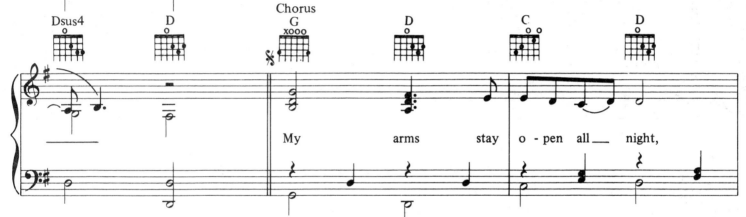

Chorus

My arms stay o - pen all_ night,

from sun - down till the morn - ing light.___ Hop - ing you can find_

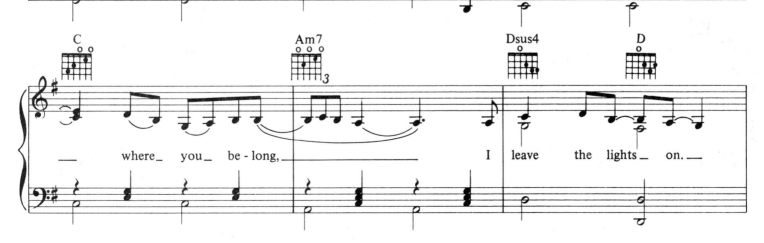

_ where_ you_ be - long,_____ I leave the lights_ on._

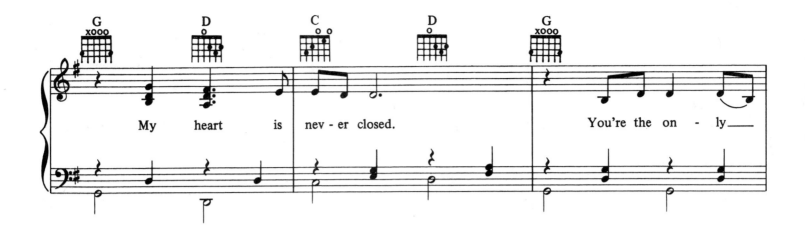

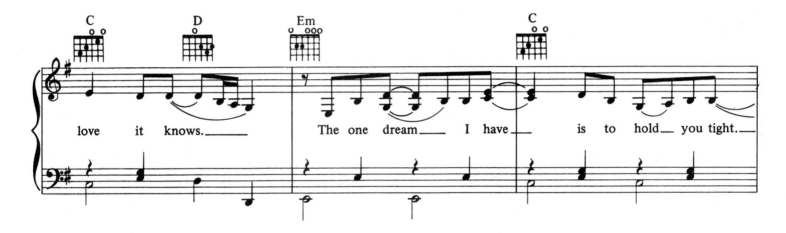

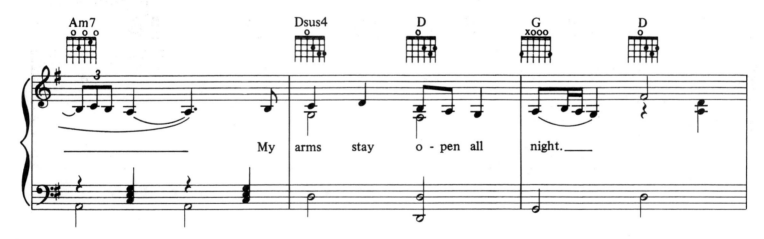

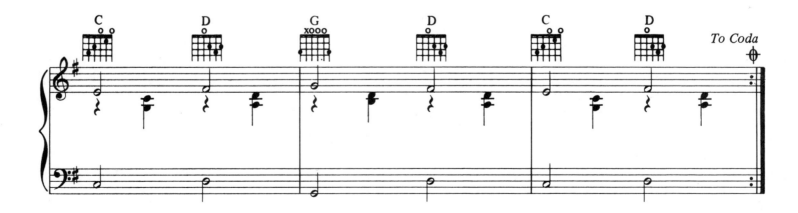

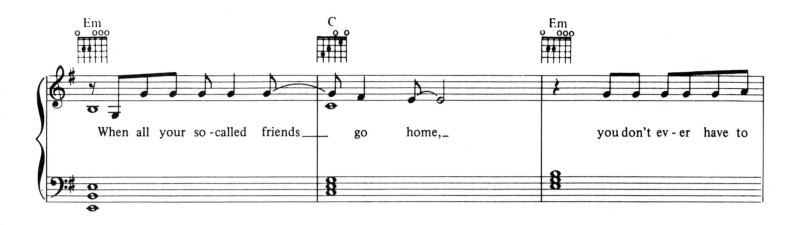

When all your so-called friends go home, you don't ev-er have to

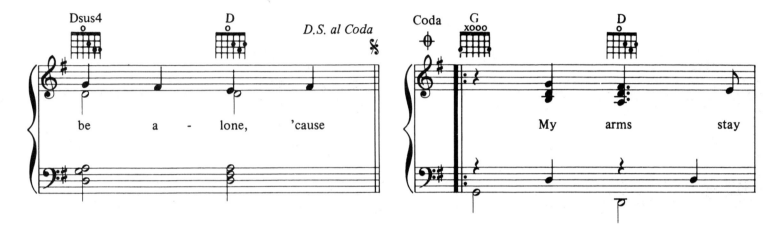

D.S. al Coda

be a - lone, 'cause

Coda

My arms stay

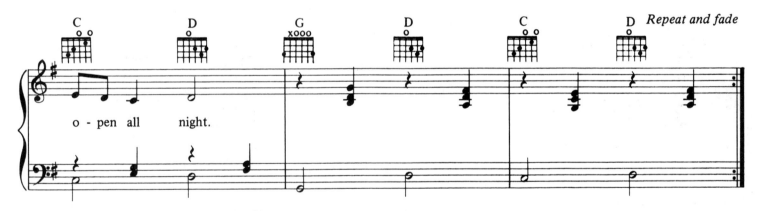

Repeat and fade

o - pen all night.

Additional Lyrics

2. Please don't think I'm crazy,
I haven't lost my mind,
But when it comes to loving you
I can always find the time.
So if it's after midnight
Or just before the break of day,
Any time you need me
It'll never be too late. *(To Chorus)*

Where've You Been

Words and Music by
Don Henry and Jon Vezner

Claire had all but giv-en up ___ when she and Ed-win
He asked her for her hand ___ for life ___ and she be-came a
Claire soon lost her mem-o-ry; ___ for-got the names of

(D.S. a tempo)

fell in ___ love. She touched his face and shook her head___ in
sales-man's ___ wife. He was home each night ___ by eight ___ but one
fam-i-ly. She nev-er spoke a word ___ a-gain. ___

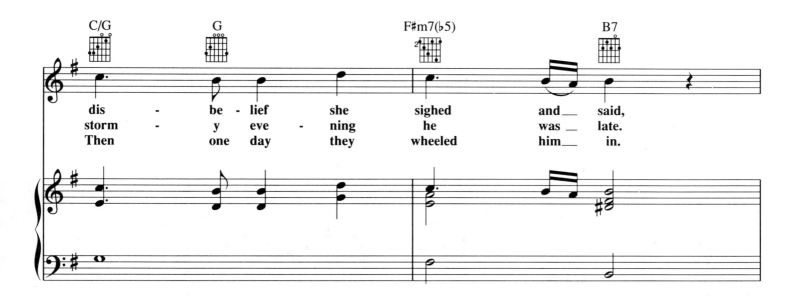

dis - be - lief she sighed and__ said,
storm - y eve - ning he was__ late.
Then one day they wheeled him__ in.

"In man - y dreams I've held_____ you near_____
Her fright - ened tears fell to_____ the floor_____
He held her hand and stroked____ her head._____

but now at last you're real - ly here."__
un - til his last key turned in_____ the door.__
In a frag - ile voice____ she said, ___ }

six - ty years she heard him snore.___ Now they're in hos -

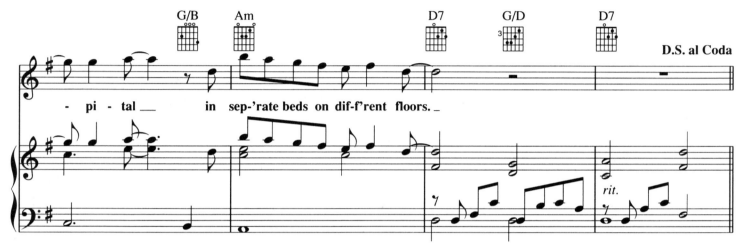

D.S. al Coda

- pi - tal ___ in sep-'rate beds on dif-f'rent floors. ___

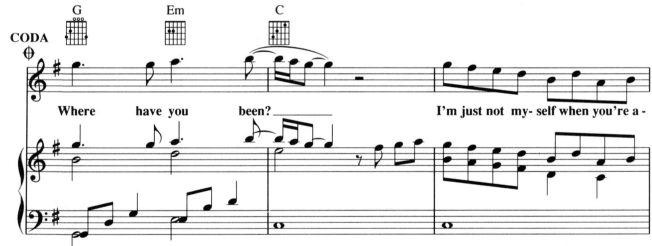

CODA

Where have you been? ___ I'm just not my- self when you're a -

way. ___ No, I'm just not my-self when you're a - way.

She Came From Fort Worth

Words and Music by
Pat Alger and Fred Koller

34

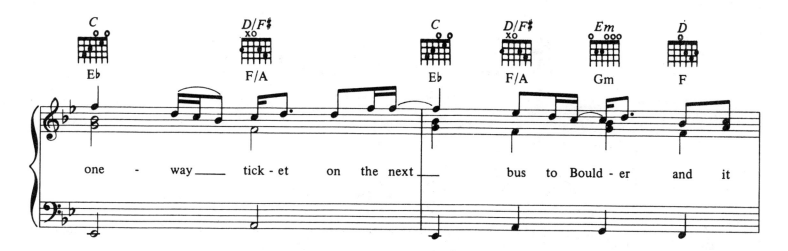

one - way ___ tick - et on the next ___ bus to Bould - er and it

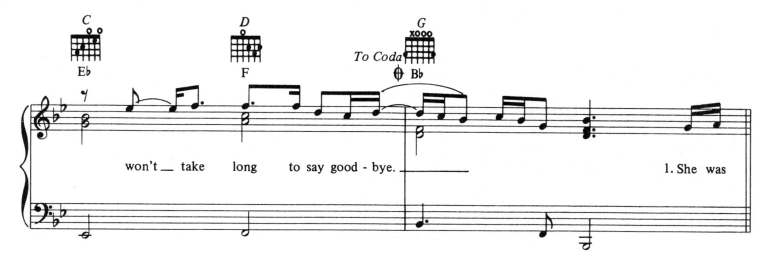

won't ___ take long to say good - bye. ___ 1. She was

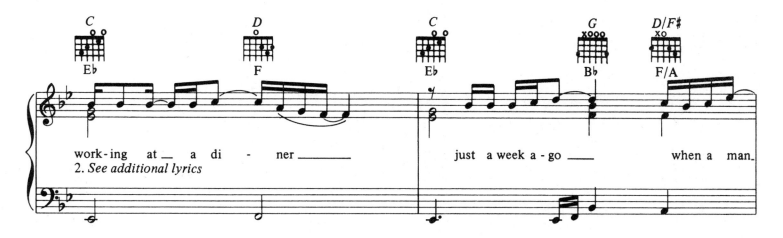

work - ing at ___ a di - ner ___ just a week a - go ___ when a man ___
2. *See additional lyrics*

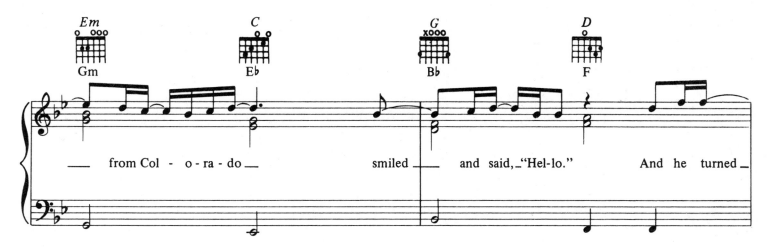

___ from Col - o - ra - do ___ smiled ___ and said, ___ "Hel-lo." And he turned ___

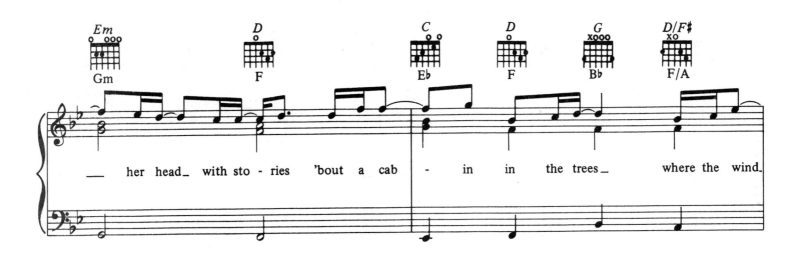

her head___ with sto - ries 'bout a cab - in in the trees___ where the wind.

___ can sing you love songs be - neath snow-capped moun - tain peaks.___

Now she's packed her fad - ed blue jeans and her

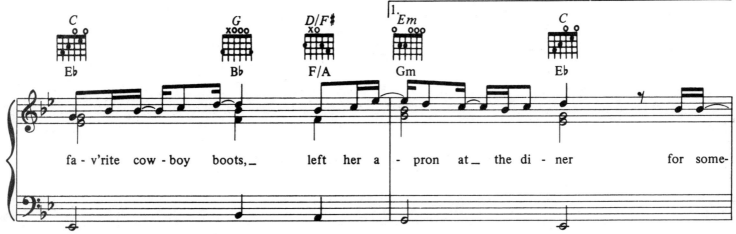

fa - v'rite cow - boy boots,___ left her a - pron at___ the di - ner for some-

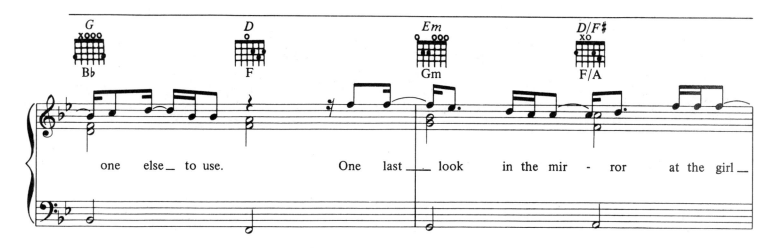

one else__ to use. One last__ look in the mir - ror at the girl__

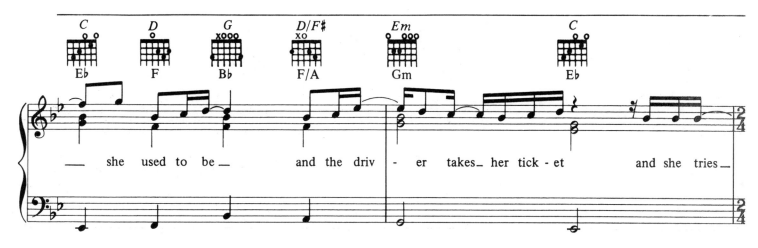

__ she used to be__ and the driv - er takes__ her tick - et and she tries__

__ to fall__ a - sleep.__ She came from

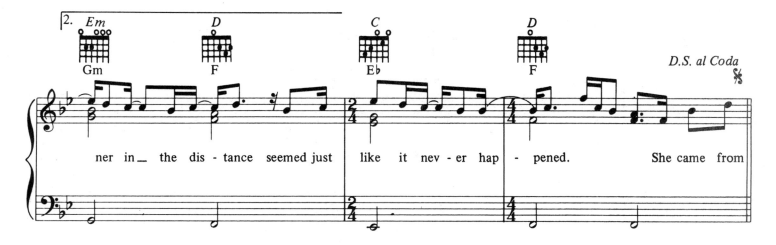

ner in__ the dis - tance seemed just like it nev - er hap - pened. She came from

D.S. al Coda

Additional Lyrics

2. And somewhere in the long dark night snow began to fall.
   Oh, the world outside was sparkling white when she heard the driver call,
   "Everyone off now for Boulder and have a real nice day."
   He was waiting on the platform and he raised his hand away.
   And she offered no resistance as he took her to his cabin,
   And that diner in the distance seemed just like it never happened. *(To Chorus)*

38

Something Of A Dreamer

Words and Music by
Mary-Chapin Carpenter

Bright country two-beat

She _ used to watch _ him from a - far. _
And she _ used to hear _ his voice at

night, _
a sweet _ whis - per

She _ used to dream _

dream - er, _____ some - thin' _ of a fool, _____

some - thin' of a heart - break, when she gives her

heart to you. _____ heart _ to you.

Lone Star State Of Mind

Words and Music by
Fred Koller, Pat Alger and Gene Levine

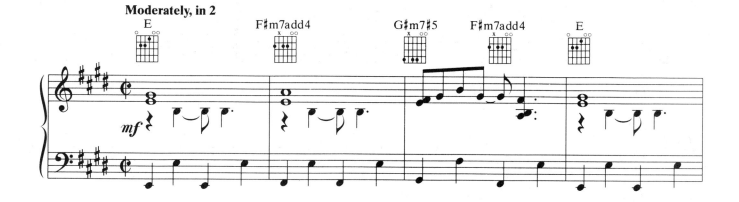

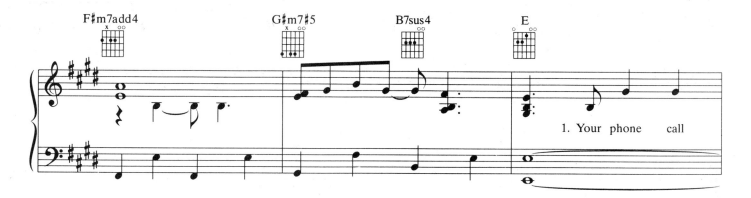

sip - pin' Cal - i - for - nia wine. ___

And I've got all ___ night to re - mem -

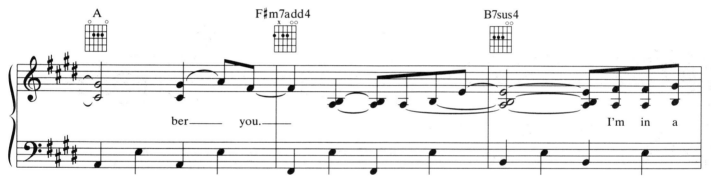

ber ___ you. ___ I'm in a

3rd time to Coda II

Lone Star ___ state of mind.

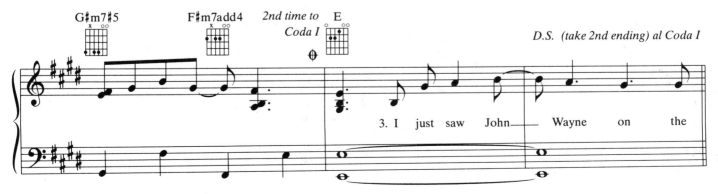

2nd time to Coda I

D.S. (take 2nd ending) al Coda I

3. I just saw John ___ Wayne on the

drew __ me to __ you and stole __ my __ heart. _____
know - ing when _ and the gift for know - ing how. _____

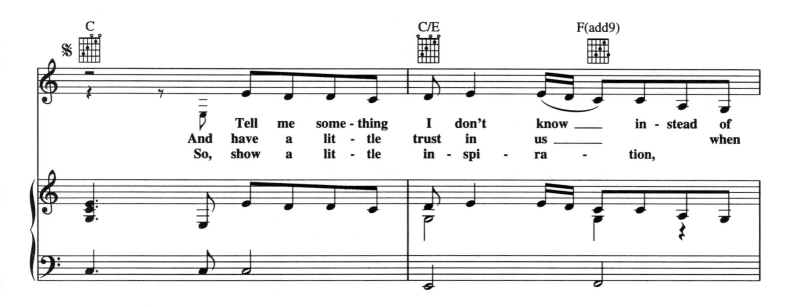

Tell me some - thing I don't know ____ in - stead of
And have a lit - tle trust in us _____ when
So, show a lit - tle in - spi - ra - tion,

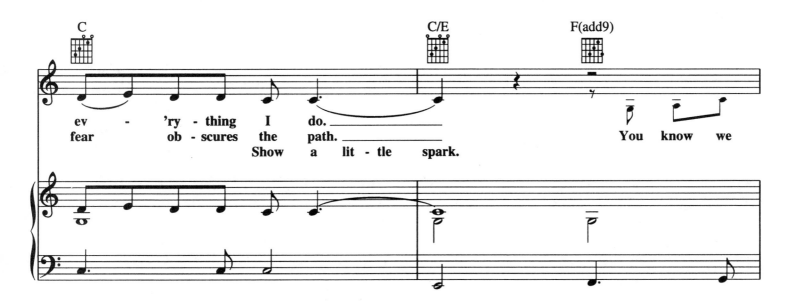

ev - 'ry - thing I do. _____
fear ob - scures the path. _____ Show a lit - tle spark. You know we

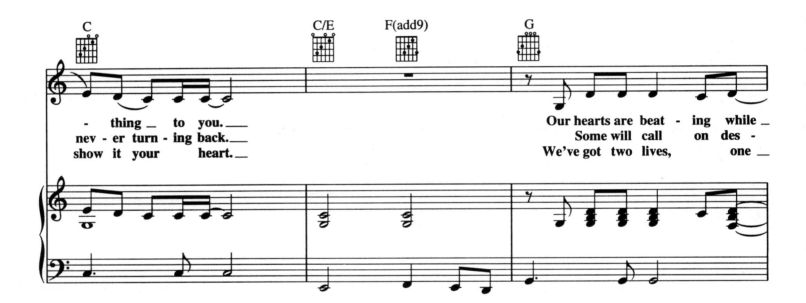

58

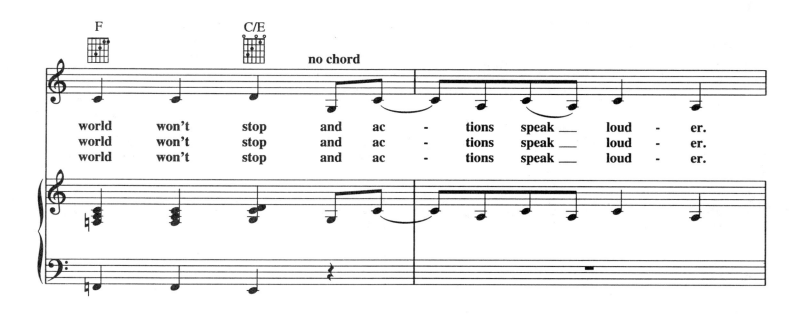

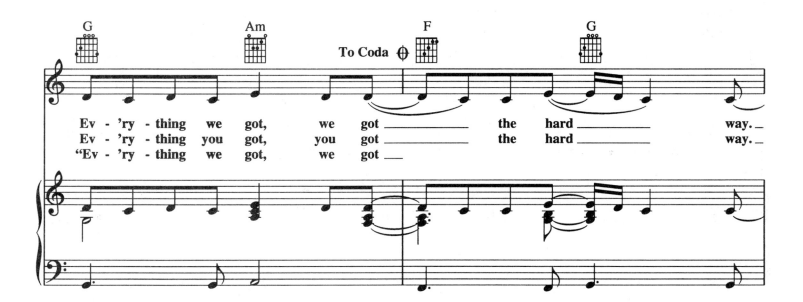

Wild One

Words and Music by
Pat Bunch, Jaime Kyle
and Will Rambeaux

Bright Country/Rock

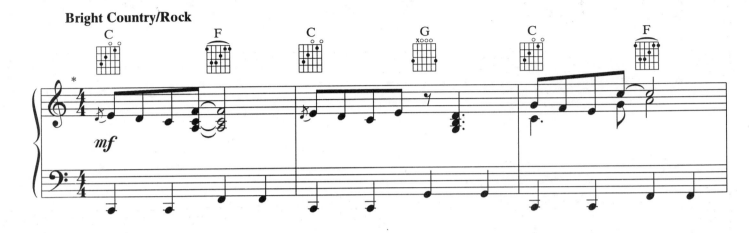

They said, "Change___ your clothes."___

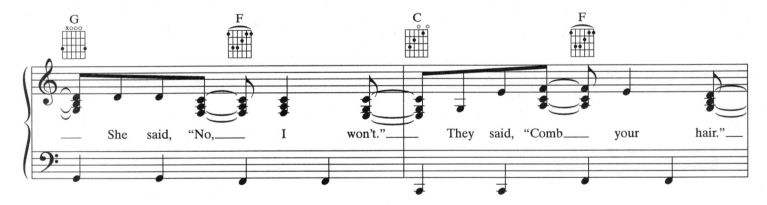

___ She said, "No,___ I won't."___ They said, "Comb___ your hair."___

___ She said, "Some___ kids don't."___ And her par - ents dreams___ went up___

in smoke.

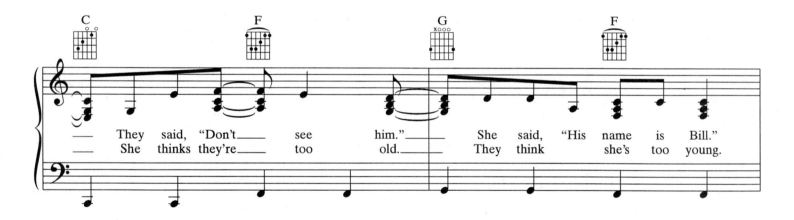

They said, "You_____ can't_____ leave."_____ She said, "Yes,_____ I_____ will."_____
She loves rock - and - roll._____ They said it's Sa - tan's_____ tongue._____

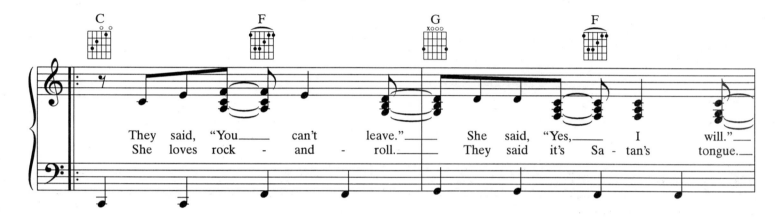

_____ They said, "Don't_____ see_____ him."_____ She said, "His name is Bill."
_____ She thinks they're_____ too_____ old._____ They think she's too young.

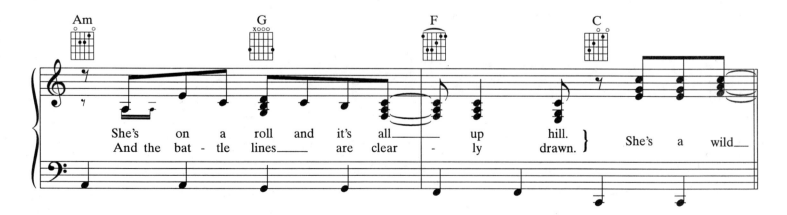

She's_____ on a roll and it's all_____ up_____ hill. } She's a wild_____
And the bat - tle lines_____ are clear - ly_____ drawn.

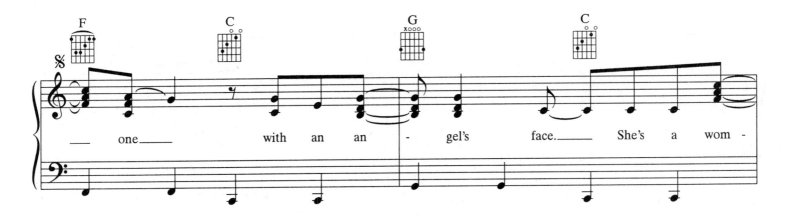

one_____ with an an - gel's face._____ She's a wom -

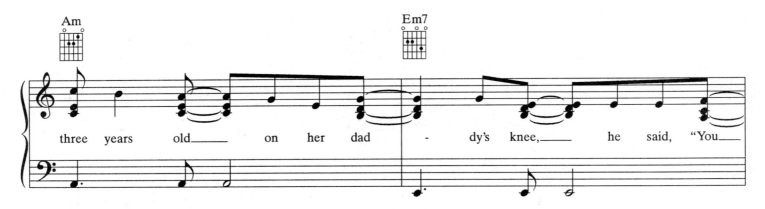

an child_____ in a state_____ of grace._____ When she was

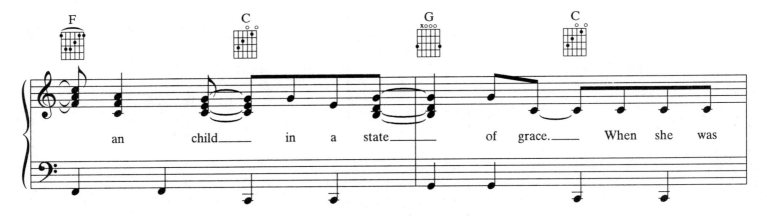

three years old_____ on her dad - dy's knee,_____ he said, "You_____

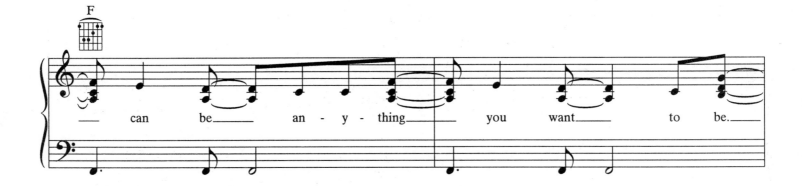

_____ can be_____ an - y - thing_____ you want_____ to be._____

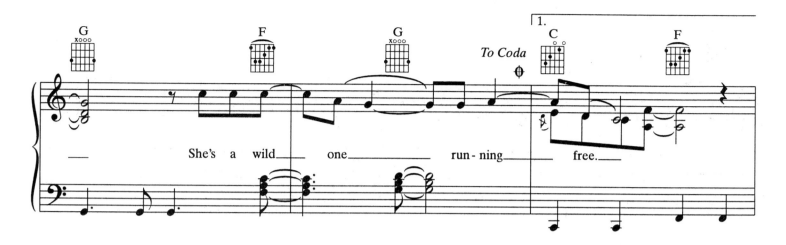

She's a wild___ one___ run - ning___ free.___

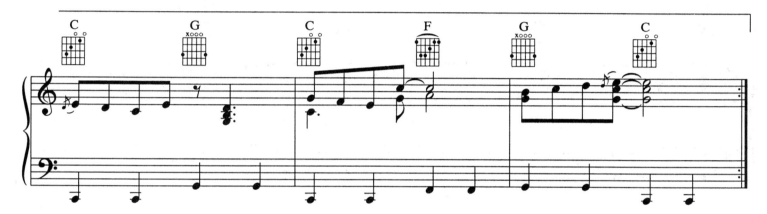

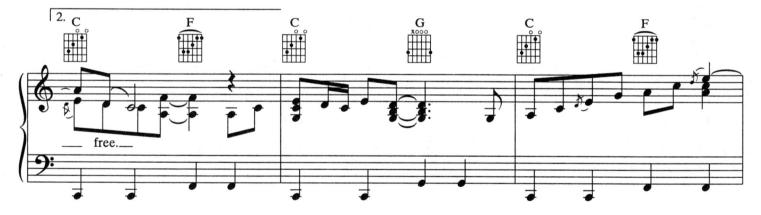

___ free.___

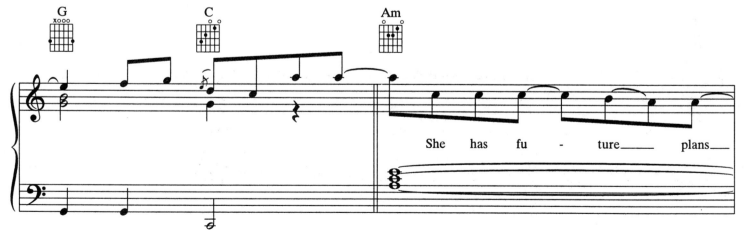

She has fu - ture___ plans___

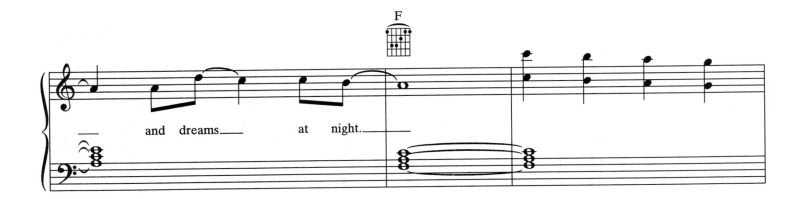

and dreams____ at night.____

When they tell her life is____ hard,____ she says, "That's____ all right."____

D.S. al Coda

____ Yeah.____ She's a wild____

Coda

____ free.____

Big Red Sun Blues

Words and Music by
Lucinda Williams

Moderately bright

1. Ev - 'ry - thing is   go - in' wrong,____

2.3. *See additional lyrics*

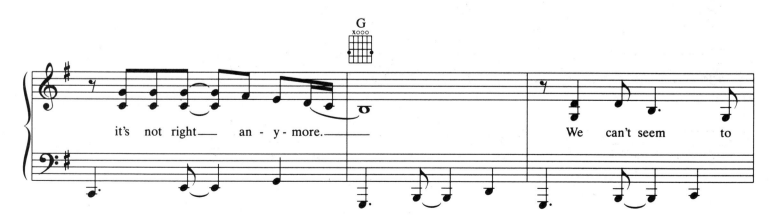

it's not right____ an - y - more.____   We   can't seem   to

Big red sun,— big red sun,— big red sun—

— blues.— 2. True love to How'm— I gon-na

Additional Lyrics

2. True love to hold
   Is worth everything.
   It's worth more than gold
   Or any diamond ring.
   But this little diamond
   And a heart that's been broken
   Are all I got from you,
   Big red sun. *(To Chorus)*

3. Look out at that western sky
   Out over the open plains.
   God only knows why
   This is all that remains.
   But give me one more promise
   And another kiss,
   And I guess the deal's still on,
   You big red sun. *(To Chorus)*

The Night's Too Long

Words and Music by
Lucinda Williams

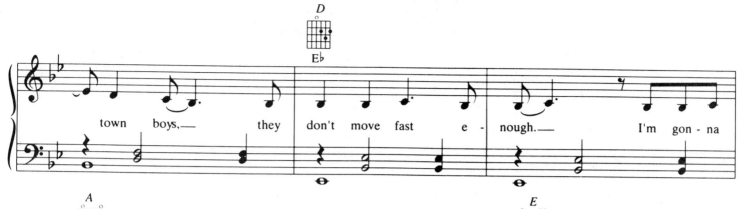

town boys,___ they don't move fast e - nough.___ I'm gon - na

find me one___ who wears a leath - er jack - et and likes his___ liv - in' rough."

___ So she saved___ her tips and o - ver-time___ and

bought an old rust - y car.___ She sold most___ ev - 'ry - thing___

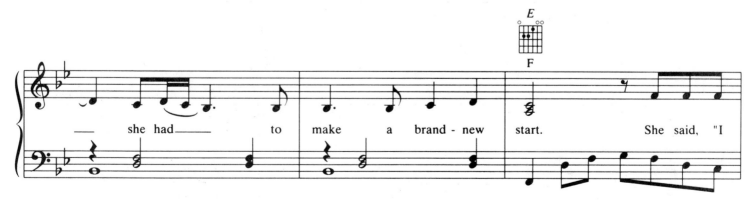

___ she had___ to make a brand - new start. She said, "I

com - in' up._____ Don't let go of her hand,_____

you just might be the right_____ man._____ She

loves_____ the night,_____ she loves_____ the night.

_____ She does - n't want the night,_____ don't want it to

end, don't want it to end. 2. Well, she

don't want it to end.

Additional Lyrics

2. Well, she works in an office now,
   And she guesses the pay's alright.
   She can buy a few new things to wear
   And still go out at night.
   And as soon as she get home from work,
   She wants to be out with a crowd
   Where she can dance and toss her head back
   And laugh out loud.

   Well, the music's playin' fast
   And they just met.
   He presses up against her,
   And his shirt's all soaked with sweat.
   And with her back against the bar,
   She can listen to the band.
   And she's holdin' a Corona,
   And it's cold against her hand. *(To Chorus)*

Crescent City

Words and Music by
Lucinda Williams

Moderately bright

Ev-'ry-bod-y's had a few,_____ now they're talk-in' a-bout
Man - de-ville._____ I can hard - ly

who knows who._____ I'm go - in' back to the Cres - cent Cit - y,_____ where
wait un - til_____ I can hear my zy - de-co_____ and *las -*

ev - 'ry-thing's still_____ the same._____ This town has said what it
siz le bon ton_____ rou - let, and take rides in

has to say._____ Now I'm af - ter that back high - way_____
o - pen cars._____ My broth - er knows where the best bars are._____

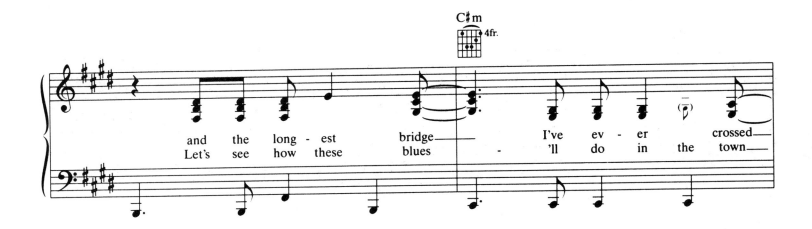

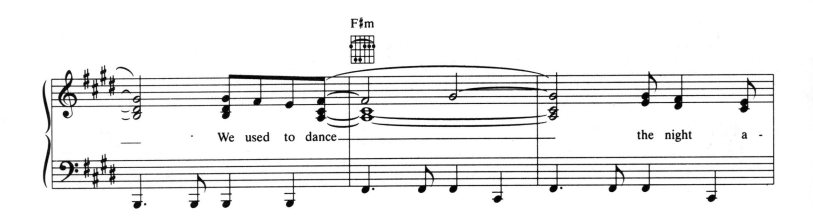

way._____ Me___ and my sis - ter,_____

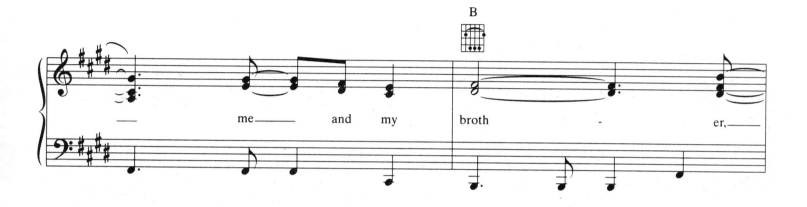

___ me___ and my broth - er,_____

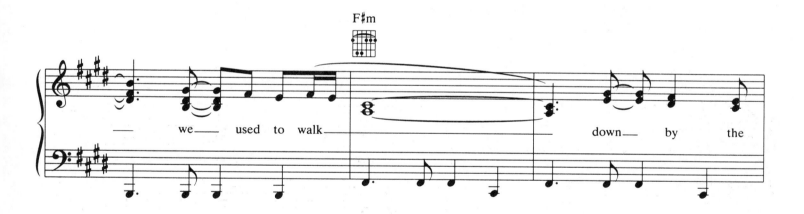

___ we used to walk_____ down___ by the

D.S. (instrumental) and fade

riv - er._____ Ma - ma lives in ___

Love Letter

Words and Music by
Bonnie Hayes

Moderately, with a funky groove

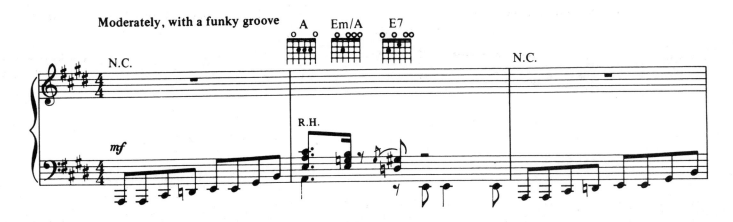

Sit - ting in front of your house,   light

rain and an ear - ly dawn.   Work - ing on a love let - ter

with the ra - di - o___ on.   Got my

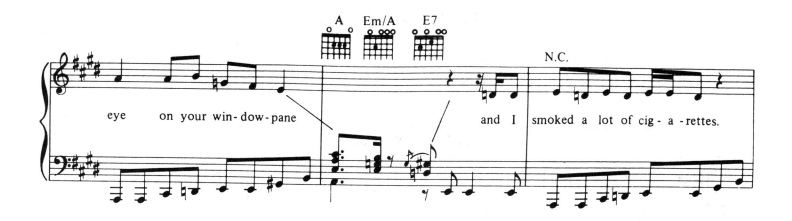

eye on your win-dow-pane and I smoked a lot of cig-a-rettes.

Mer-cy, mer-cy, but love is strange and you

have-n't e-ven kissed me yet. We come to push,

push comes to shove,_ shove comes to touch,_ touch will come to love._

We come to push,   push comes to shove,—

shove comes to touch,—   touch will come to love.—   Love   don't sit wait-ing.

Love   don't be-have.—   Love's wait-ing in the car—   in the pour-ing rain.— I'm—

D.S. al Coda

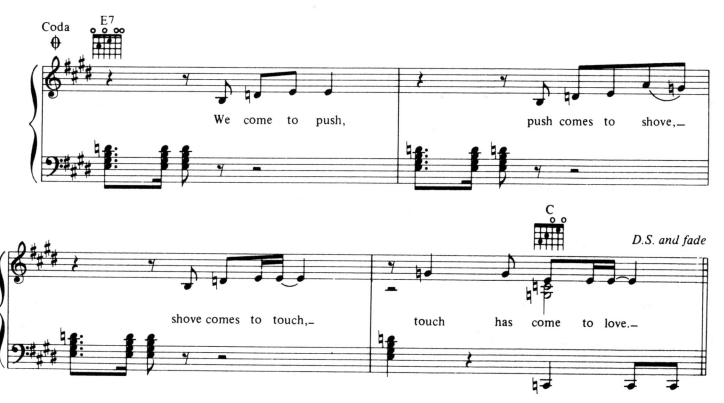

Coda

We come to push,   push comes to shove,—

D.S. and fade

shove comes to touch,—   touch has come to love.—

Seeds

Words and Music by
Pat Alger and Ralph Murphy

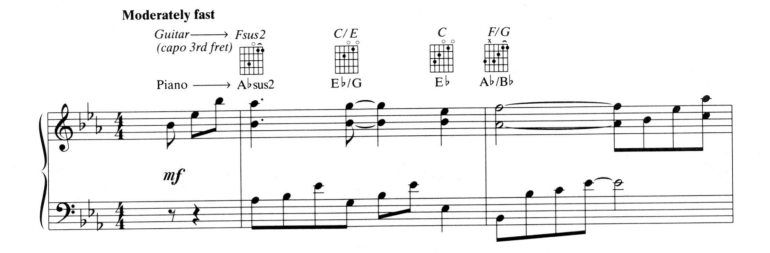

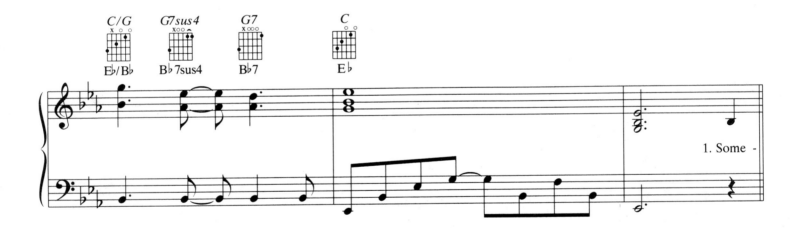

times I stop____ on my way home____ to watch the chil - dren play,____

2. *See additional lyrics*

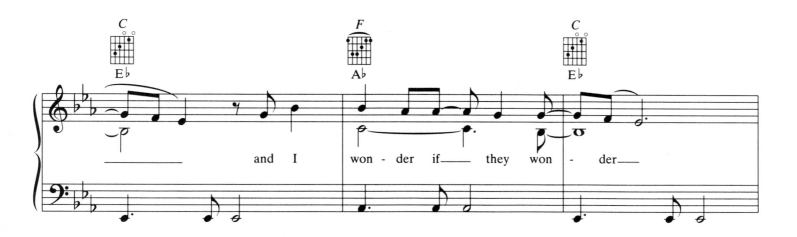

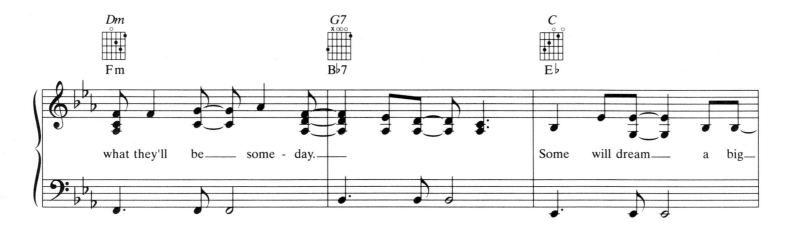

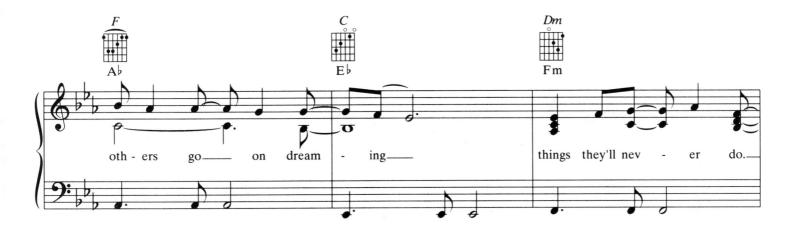

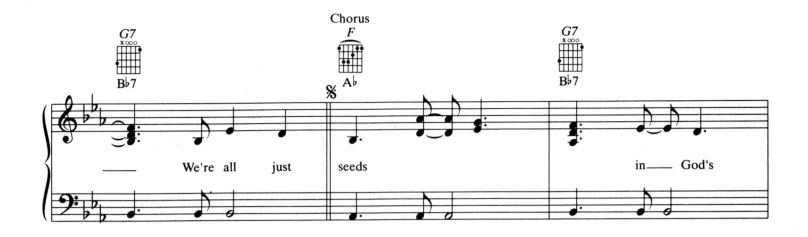

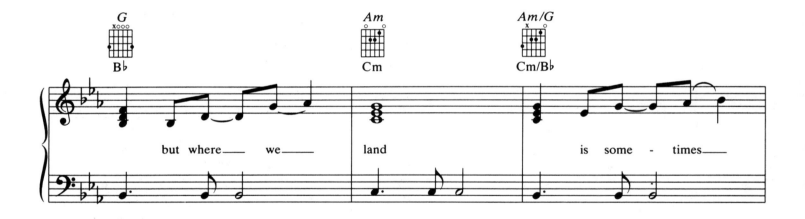

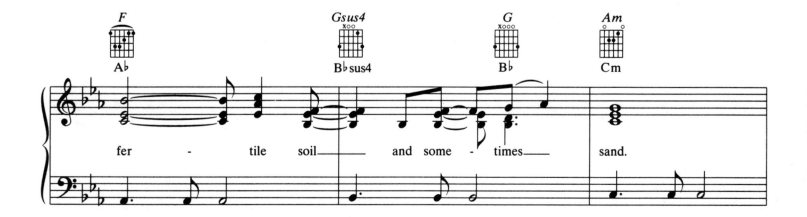

90

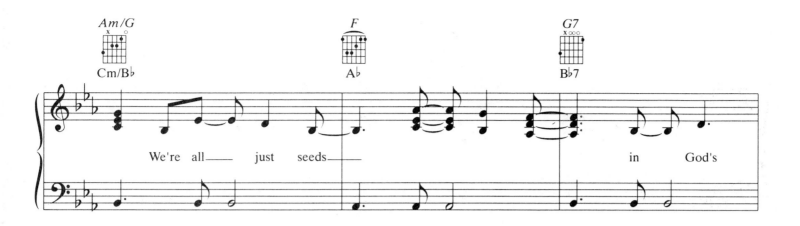

We're all___ just seeds___ in God's

hands.

1.

To Coda ⊕

2.

And as I'm stand-ing at___ the cross-

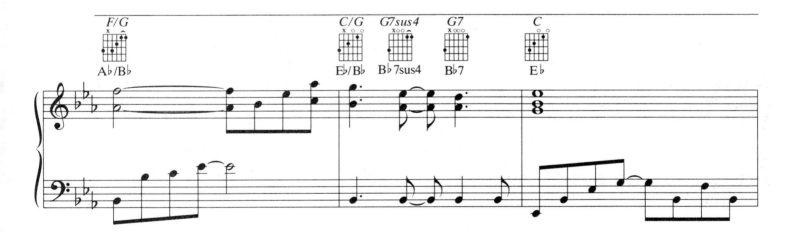

91

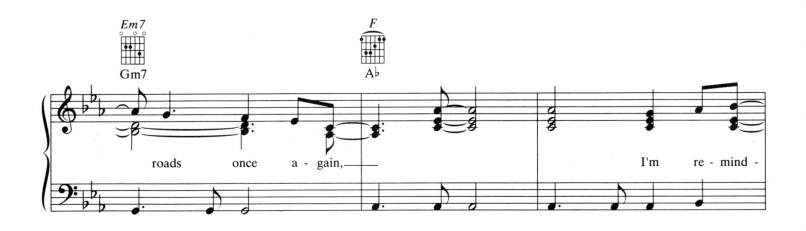

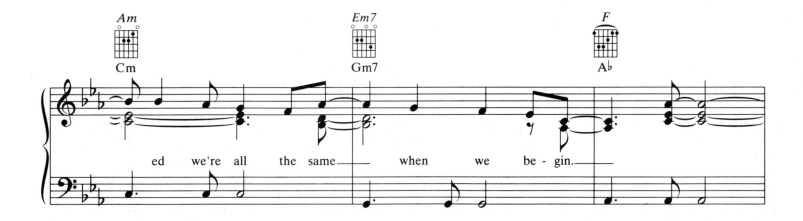

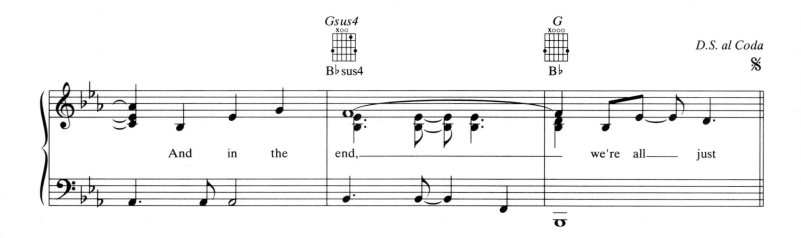

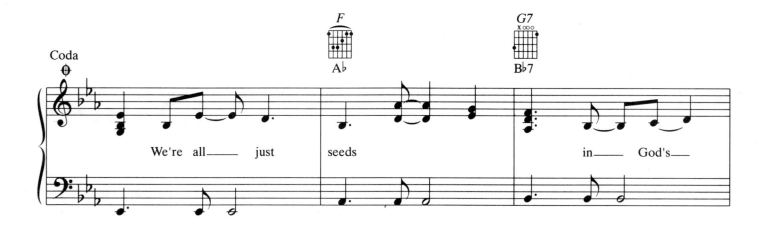

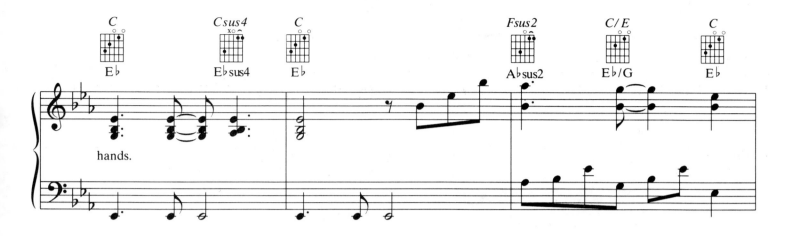

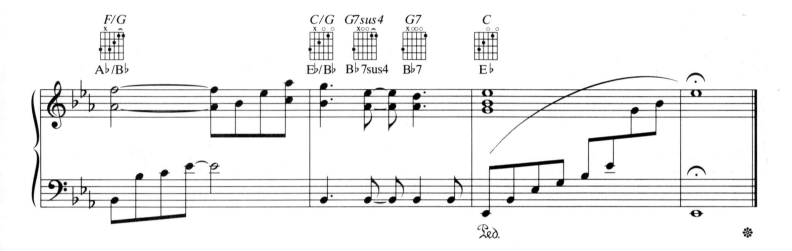

Additional Lyrics

2. I saw a friend the other day I hardly recognized;
   He'd done a lot of livin' since I last looked in his eyes.
   And he told his tale of how he'd failed and the lessons he'd been taught,
   But he offered no excuses, and he left me with this thought: *(To Chorus)*

Trainwreck Of Emotion

Words and Music by
Jon Vezner and Alan Rhody

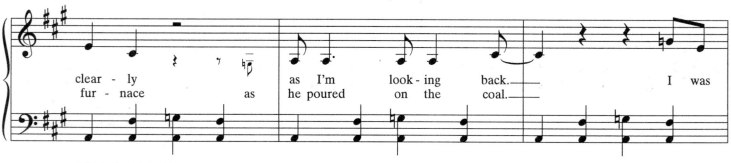

* Recorded a half step lower.

head-ed down__ the wrong__ way__ on a one-way track.
Drive wheel__ churn - ing,__ I mean love was on__ a roll.

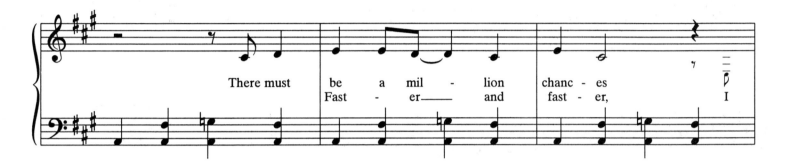

There must be a mil - lion chanc - es
Fast - er__ and fast - er, I

that a fool__ could take.__ Well, this fool took
swear we left__ the ground.__ But when that smoke had

ev - 'ry one__ and nev - er hit the brakes.__ I'm
cleared, he was__ no-where a - round.__

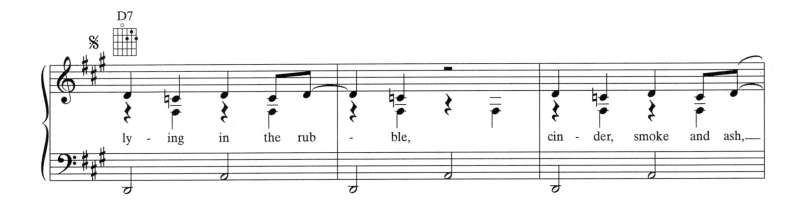

ly - ing in the rub - ble, cin - der, smoke and ash,——

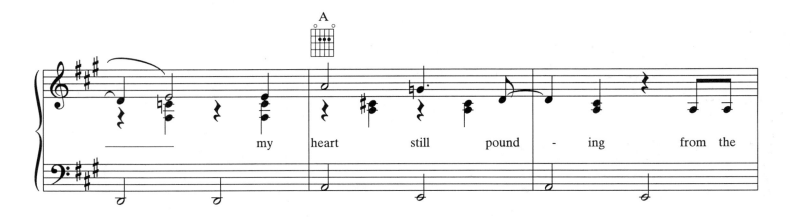

—————— my heart still pound - ing from the

im - pact of the crash.—— I can see to - mor - row's head -

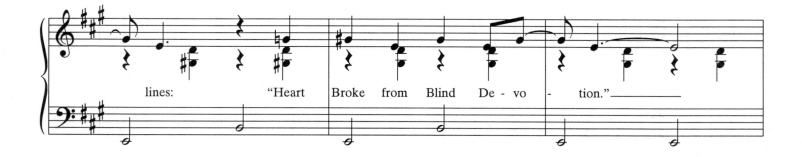

lines: "Heart Broke from Blind De - vo - tion."——————

and left me de - railed. _____ I'm

Just one more vic - tim of a

train - wreck of e - mo - tion. _____

Train - wreck of e - mo-

Repeat and fade

tion. _____ Train-wreck of e - mo-

Like We Never Had A Broken Heart

Words and Music by
Pat Alger and Garth Brooks

Slow Country Ballad

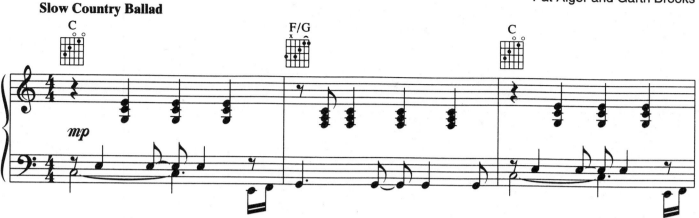

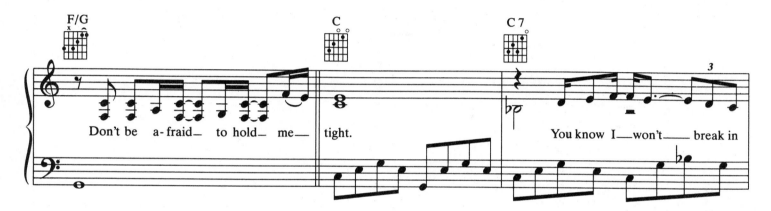

Don't be a-fraid— to hold— me— tight.   You know I—won't— break in

two.   What we're do-ing here— to-night____

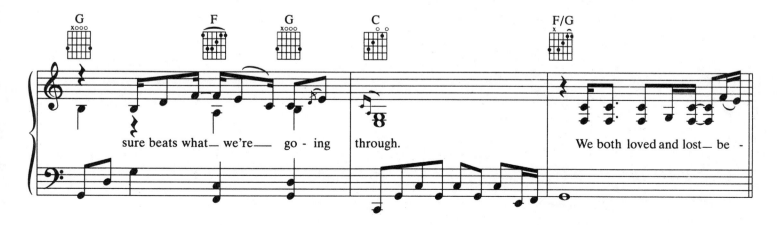

sure beats what— we're— go-ing through.   We both loved and lost— be -

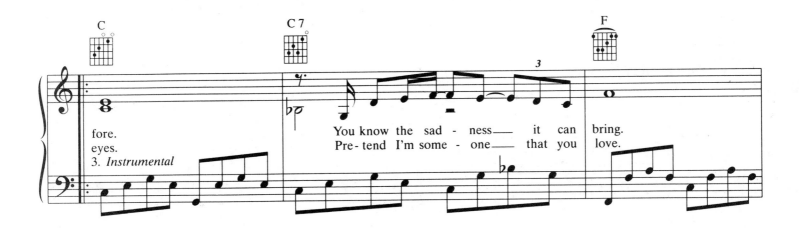

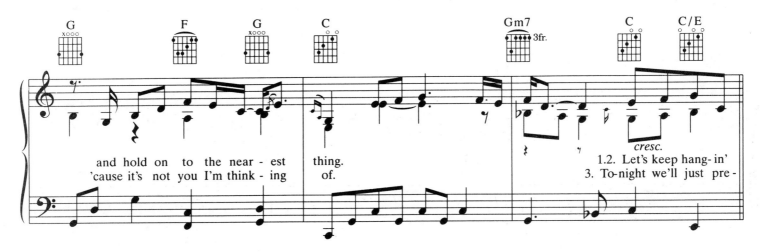

Let's make love ___ to-night ___
Let's make love ___ a- gain ___ }

like we nev-er had a ___ bro-ken

1.2.

heart.
dim.
mp

Don't be a-fraid ___ to close ___ your ___
Instrumental

3.

heart.

Oh, let's make love ___ a- gain ___

like we nev-er had a ___ bro-ken

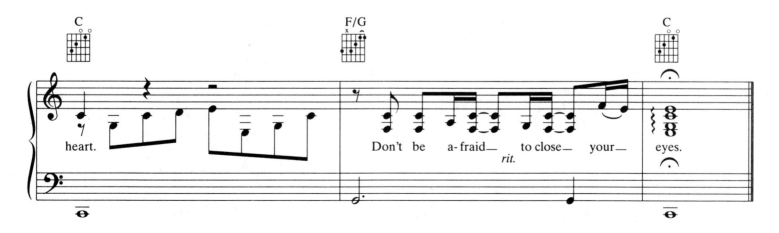

heart.

Don't be a-fraid ___ to close ___ your ___ eyes.
rit.

God Will

Words and Music by
Lyle Lovett

102

And who keeps on say - ing___
that he still___ wants you___ when you're through___
run - ning a - round?___ And
who keeps on lov - ing___ you___ when you've been ly -
says he'll for - give___ you___ and says that he'll

God will but I won't and that's the dif - ference be - tween God and

me.

So who

tween God and me.

How Can I Help You To Say Goodbye

Words and Music by
Burton Banks Collins and Karen Taylor-Good

Moderately slow

1. Through the back— win - dow of our fif - ty-nine— wag - on,— I

2.3. *See additional lyrics*

watched my best— friend Ja - mie slip-pin' fur - ther a - way.—

I kept on wav - in'___ till I could-n't___ see___ her.___ And

through my tears___ I asked a - gain___ why we could-n't stay.

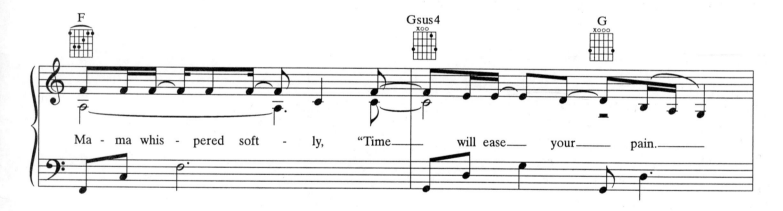

Ma - ma whis - pered soft - ly, "Time___ will ease___ your___ pain.___

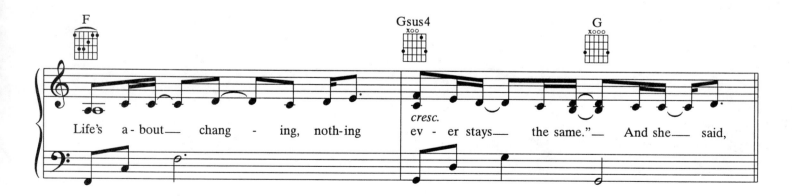

Life's a - bout___ chang - ing, noth-ing *cresc.* ev - er stays___ the same." And she___ said,

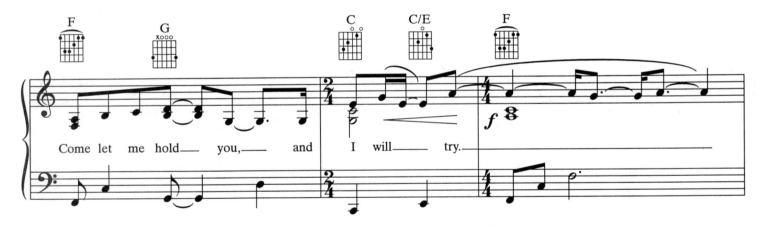

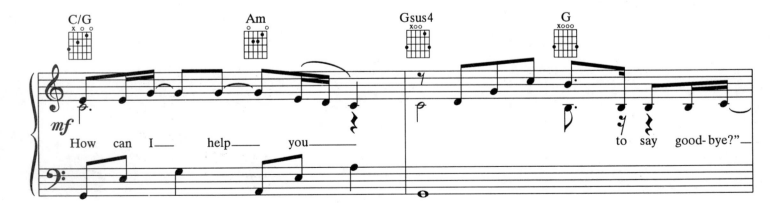

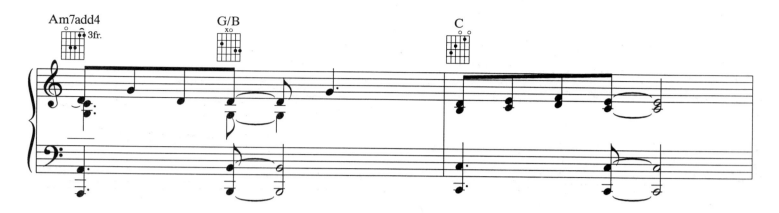

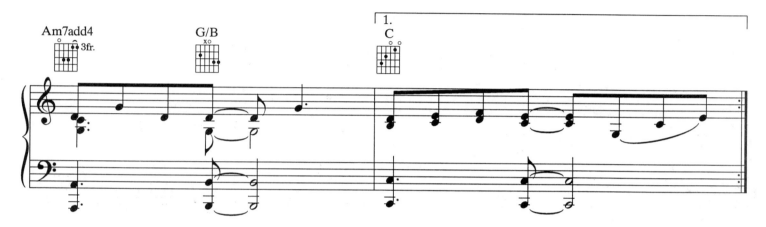

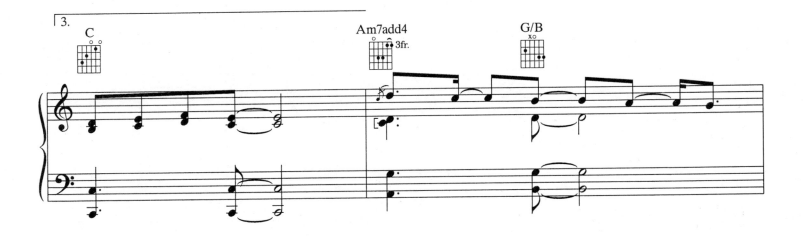

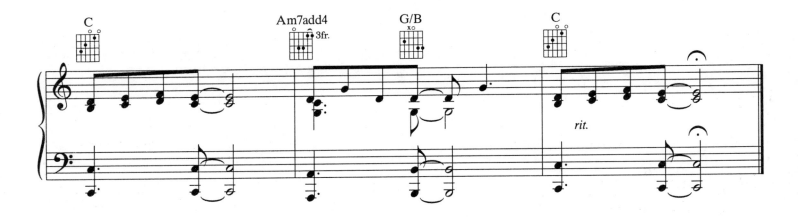

Additional Lyrics

2. I sat on our bed, he packed his suitcase.
   I held a picture of our wedding day.
   His hands were trembling. We both were crying.
   He kissed me gently, and then he quickly walked away.
   I called up mama. She said "Time will ease your pain.
   Life's about changing. Nothing ever stays the same."
   And she said, *(To Chorus)*

3. Sittin' with mama alone in her bedroom,
   She opened her eyes and then squeezed my hand.
   She said, "I have to go now, my time here is over."
   And with her final words she tried to help me understand.
   Mama whispered softly, "Time will ease your pain.
   Life's about changing. Nothing ever stays the same."
   And she said, *(To Chorus)*

Part Of Me

Words and Music by
Tony Arata

Slow Country Ballad

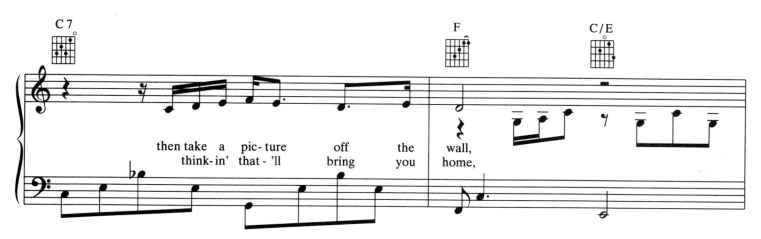

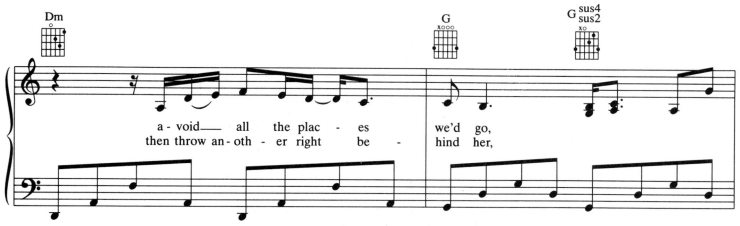

111

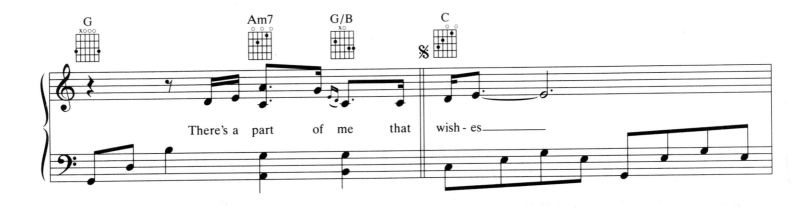

There's a part of me that wish-es____

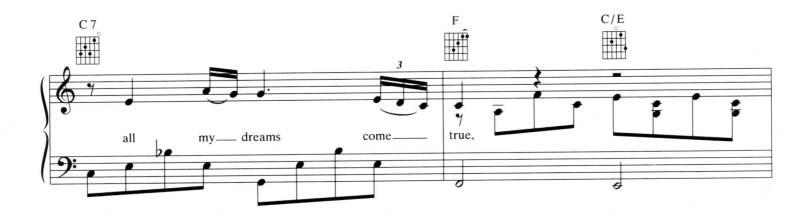

all my____ dreams come____ true,

and a part of me that prays____ that I'll wake up____ some -

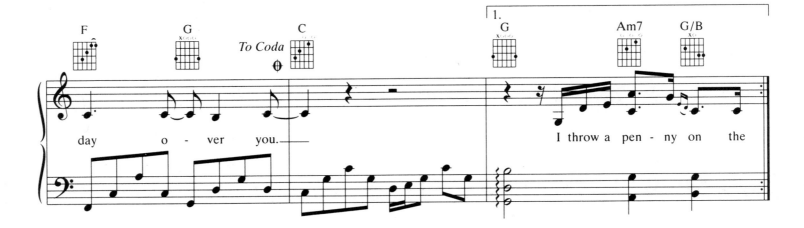

day o - ver you.____

I throw a pen - ny on the

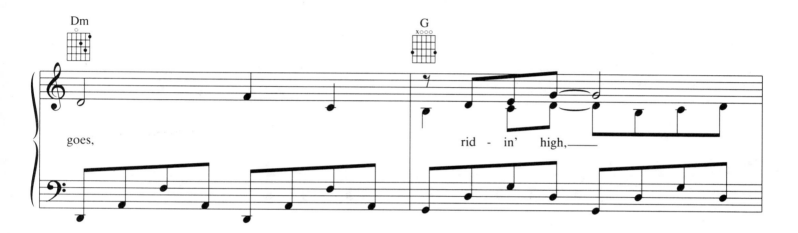

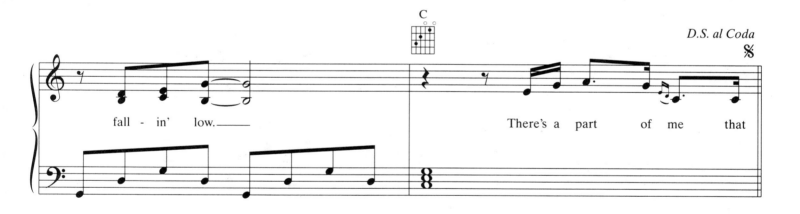

Goin' Gone

Words and Music by
Fred Koller, Pat Alger
and Bill Dale

Moderately bright, gently

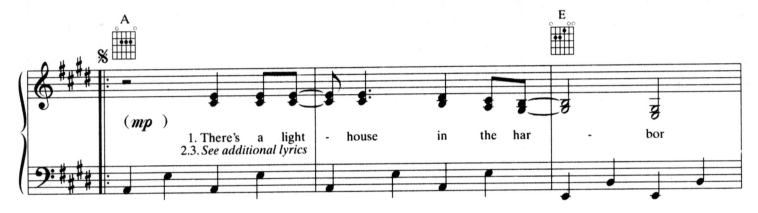

no one to re - turn_____ to_____

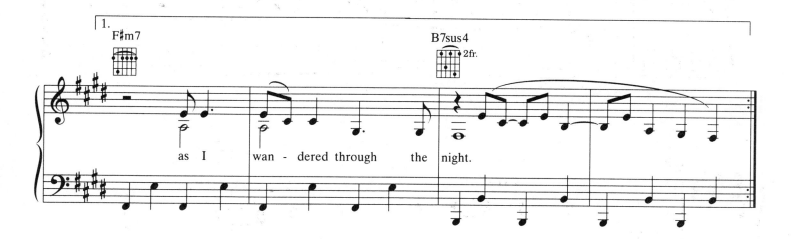

1. F#m7   B7sus4   2fr.

as I wan - dered through the night.

2. F#m7   B7sus4   2fr.

and I would look___ for love___ no more.___

cresc.

Chorus
A   E

Deep in the wa - ters___ of___ love I am

mf

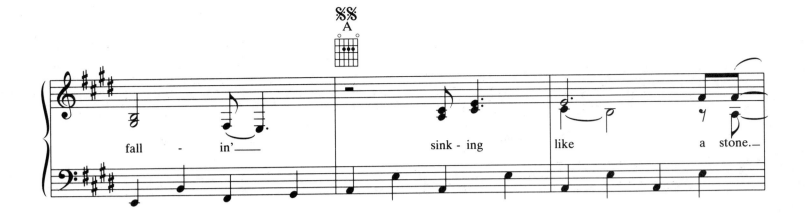

fall - in'__ sink - ing like a stone.__

Deep in my__

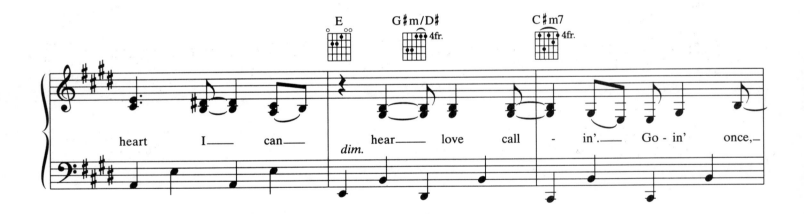

heart I__ can__ *dim.* hear__ love call - in'.__ Go - in' once,__

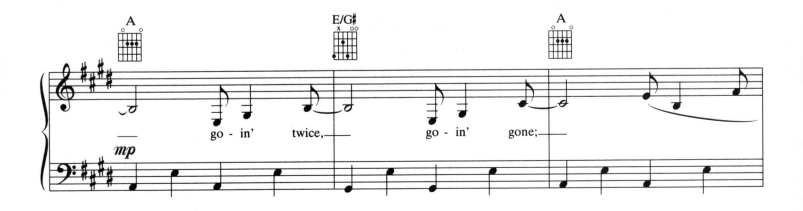

mp go - in' twice,__ go - in' gone;__

go - in' once,   go - in' twice,   go - in'_____

cresc.

gone.

mf

dim.

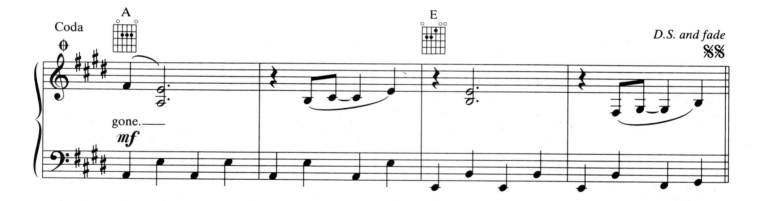

Coda

gone._____

mf

Additional Lyrics

2. From the first time that I saw you
   Standing silent by the shore,
   I knew my search was over,
   And I would look for love no more. *(To Chorus)*

3. There's a ship on the horizon
   Makin' its way against the wind.
   Fom the place where I stand watchin',
   I swear my ship is comin' in. *(To Chorus)*

You Lie

Words and Music by
Austin Roberts, Charlie Black
and Bobby Fischer

'Til

you can find a way to say____ good - bye, you

lie. _____

do.

Oh, ___ but you don't _ know,

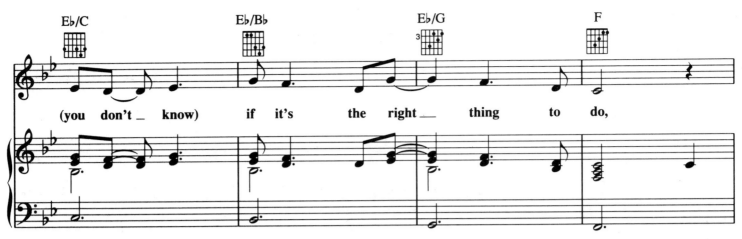

(you don't __ know) if it's the right __ thing to do,

D.S.S. al Coda II

so you

CODA II

bye, oh you

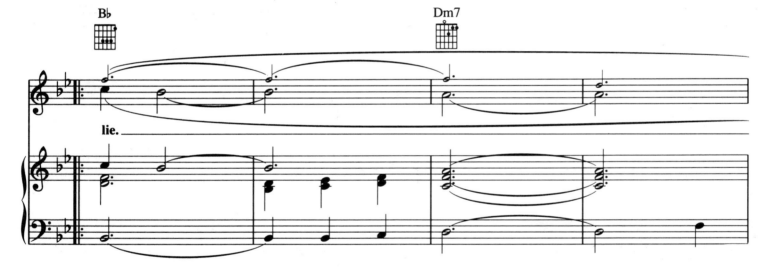

lie. ___

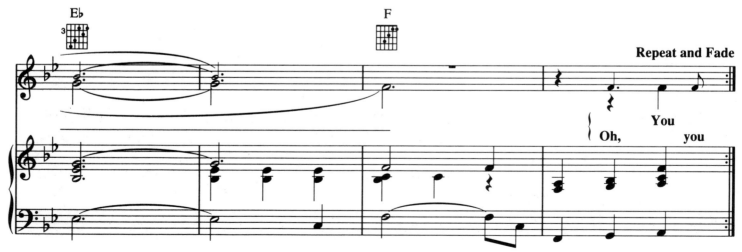

Repeat and Fade

You
Oh, you you

I Hear A Call

Words and Music by
Tony Arata

I hear a call,_____ how will I an-

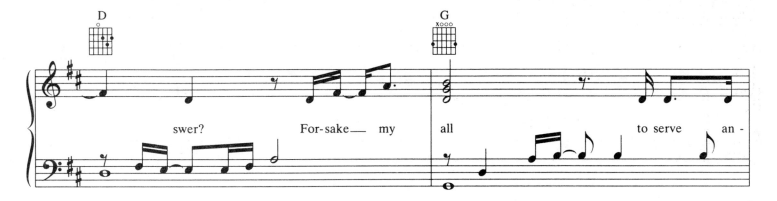

swer? For-sake__ my all to serve an-

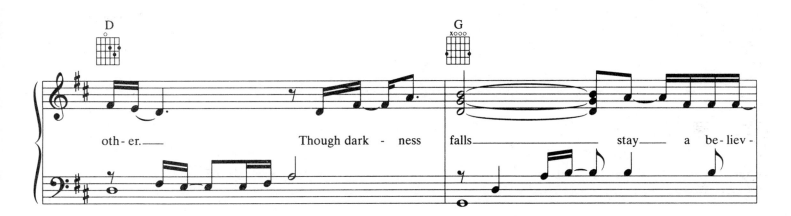

oth-er.____ Though dark - ness falls____ stay__ a be-liev-

er._____ I hear a call,_____ now will I an -

swer.

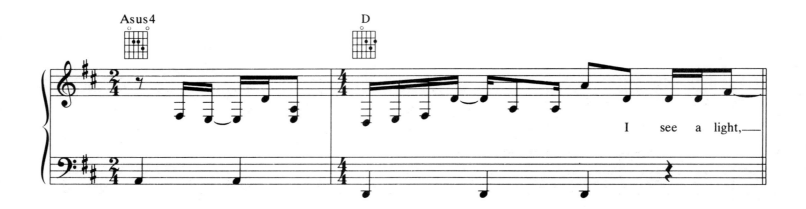

I see a light,_____

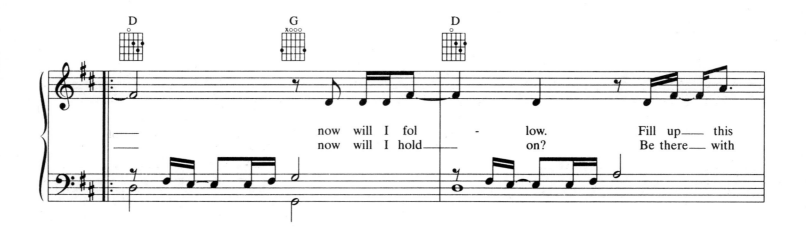

_____ now will I fol _____ - low. Fill up_____ this
_____ now will I hold_____ on? Be there_____ with

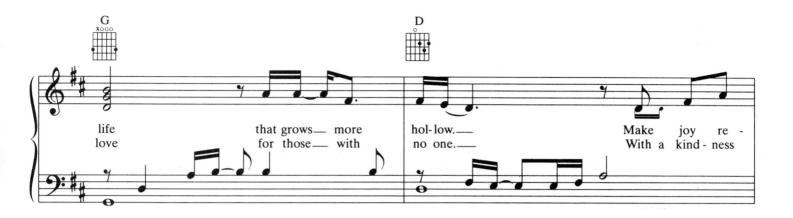

life _____ that grows—— more hol-low.——   Make joy re -
love _____ for those—— with no one.——   With a kind - ness

side _____ where there—— lives sor - row.——   I see a light,——
such _____ it lives—— though I'm gone.——   I feel a touch,——

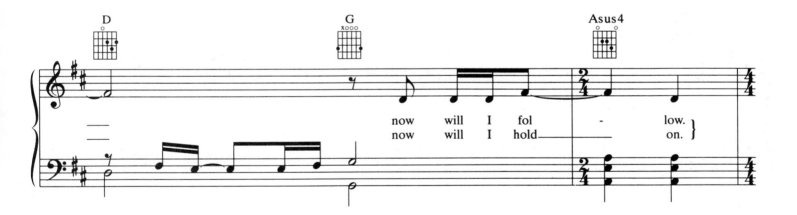

now will I fol - low. }
now will I hold _____ on. }

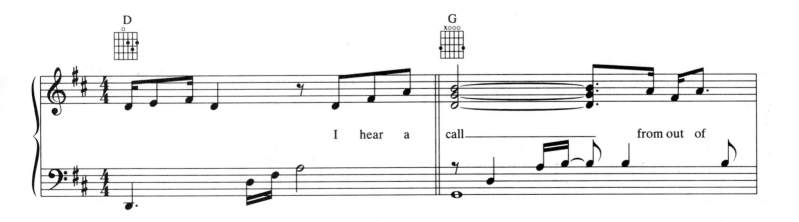

I hear a call _____ from out of

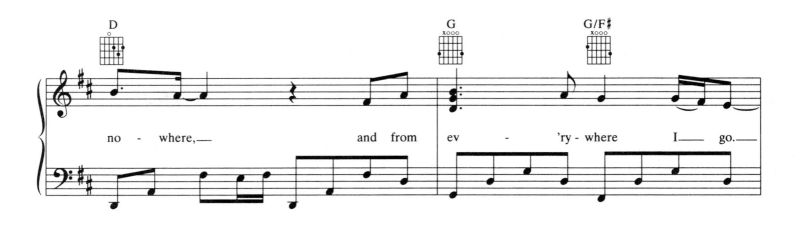

no - where,____ and from ev - 'ry - where I__ go.

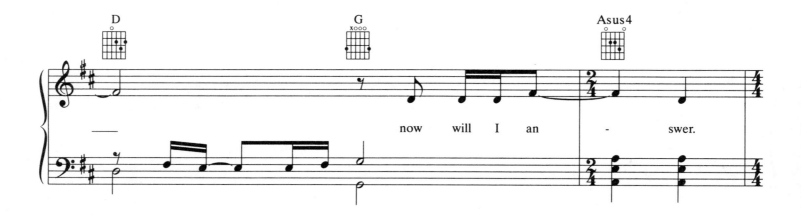

I feel a touch____ I hear a call,__

now will I an - swer.

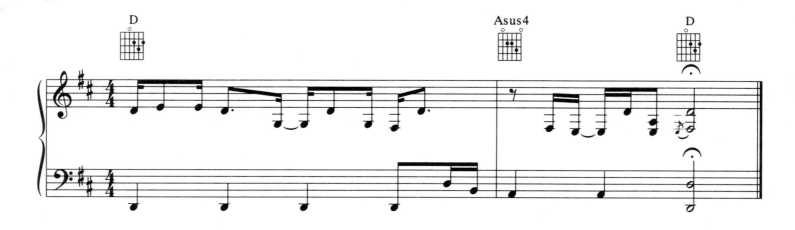